Dad Jokes

— 〰 —

Father's Day Edition

Copyright © 2018 by Try Not to Laugh Challenge Joke Group

ALL RIGHTS RESERVED. By purchase of this book, you have been licensed one copy for personal use only. No part of this work may be reproduced, redistributed, or used in any form or by any means without prior written permission of the publisher and copyright owner.

THINK YOU CAN WIN OUR DAD JOKE CONTEST ?!?

Try Not to Laugh Challenge is having a CONTEST to see who has the BEST DAD JOKE in all of America!

Please email us your best **original** joke and you could win a

Exotic Meats Crate worth $100!

INSIDE THE BOX:

Cured & Cultured:
Venison, Wild Boar, Biltong Beef, Elk, Buffalo, and Alligator Jerky

Safari Sticks:
Pheasant, Maple Duck, Ostrich, and Alligator Jerky Sticks.

Here are the rules:

1. It must be funny. Please do not give us jokes that aren't funny. We get enough of those from our joke writers

2. It must be original. We have computers and we know how to use them.

Email your best joke to:

tntlpublishing@gmail.com

Winner will be announced via email
GOOD LUCK!

Try Not to Laugh Challenge Group

Dad Jokes

Happy Father's Day!

Your mother solves problems much like the Pharos of the Egyptian days. Just throws pain and human suffering at it until I get it done.

Why do unpopular teams play in hotter arenas?
Because they have no fans.

If I had a nickel for every time you were an idiot, I'd have one nickel because it's a permanent condition.

I didn't learn about the dangers of lead poisoning until after your sister.

I have a pain in my back, and I keep telling it to go away, but your still here talking to me.

I like a lot of things! Beer, fishing with beer and golfing with brandy!

It's worth $50 to get your mother a gift card, $2 for the card to put it in, but the couch you have to sleep on the next week? Priceless.

You know it's a good beer if it comes in a bottle. Or a can. Or if it's beer.

I'm not always right, but the percentages are so high, you might as well take my word for gospel.

If I ever start to lose my mind, do me a favor. Put your mother in a home. That should buy me a few more years.

Are we at the store? Because she was definitely checking me out.

Do you know how much a hook and a peg leg costs?
An arm and a leg.

If dolphins are so smart, why haven't they invented anything?
It's all that seaweed

Did you hear about the kidnapping?
I hope he woke up.

How can you tell a snowman's gender?
Snowballs

Why is Superman so much stronger than I am?
He was a little meteor.

I garden because it's like music to me...
I've got all the best beets.

If you milked an elk and turned it into cream, you could call it moose!

I had myself a gorgeous catch back in the day. 120lb's, skin was as smooth as silk, truly top of the line catch...She's stuck around and picked up a few pounds since then.

What do you call a tour bus with a bomb on it?
A tour-pedo.

Happy Birthday! Today you can celebrate the greatest achievement of your life!
You existing.

Men spoon, women snuggle, and couples snooze.

My Fitbit complains to me I don't walk far enough each day. I'm going to have to start taking steps to avoid that.

I get brain freeze all the time. Every time we talk really.

Sexual education is a joke
in this country.
I didn't learn about the importance of
condoms until after you were born!

Why do cars hum?
Because they can't pronounce
the words

I am made of leather, spend my days
walking the streets, and people address
me by telling me to leave. What am I?
A Shoe!

The police confiscated all the illegal Viagra. The news praised them as a hardened task force.

A pile of wood spends its whole life looking for its match.

He liked to cuddle with the money he got from the bank. I wanted to send him to the hospital, but apparently its legal tender.

If you cut off a chickens head, it can walk around for a few minutes before it dies. If you cut off his legs, it can't.

Like bananas, I'm super appealing.

I don't eat ranch dressing. Cowboy clothing tastes terrible.

Google is the worst. I tried to look for a tiki torch, but they only gave me 200,000,000 matches.

I wanted to write a duck joke, but it kept quacking me up.

I was going to tell a constipation joke, but I couldn't get it out!

A paper dress would be tear-able.

Every time I look in the mirror I see the smart and handsome 18-year-old man I once was. I can't see wrinkles without my glasses.

Did you miss me?
Yeah, but I'll get another chance when I drive tomorrow.

What do you call a famous parrot?
A celebirdy

That's a nice camera! I heard if you see the flash from a canon it can kill you!

Jungle cats never stay faithful. They are all cheetahs.

What do you call shoes chipped out of ice?
Slippers.

I don't procrastinate. Whatever I could do today I can do better tomorrow.

I had a party for the Apollo launch! It was a blast...

The golden rule is very important. Keep an empty urinal between each man.

We can't have nice things because that's your mom's job.

Don't let anyone ever tell you that you're not beautiful. It's rude, and they don't need to point it out.

I'll cry the day you get married. It'll be painful to write every check. I'd fight you for the check, but you'd win and I'd have to pay anyways.

We spent your inheritance on the college education you don't use, the wedding you annulled, and a lot of lube so we can try again.

You can be anything you want when you grow up, and whenever you want to grow up just let me know.

Can you stitch?
Because that body is ripped.

Where did the corn go on vacation?
Cape cob.

What kind of dog doesn't work out?
A husky.

My Halloween party is a hit. People are just dying to get in!

One peanut teased another because he was salty.

First, a priest blesses the holy water; then he boils the hell out of it.

I'm not cocky, I'm conceited. Cocky is when you're not amazing.

Let's get this party started, let's rage! Where's the croquet set?

I'm not lazy! Just resting up for a day I might need to do something.

What does the man who has been divorced three times keep doing wrong?
He keeps getting married.

It's pretty easy to keep a marriage healthy and happy for a long time.
Drink together, often.

What is a procrastinating lizard called?
The drag-on.

How many grapes grow on the vine?
All of them

What did the Xmas tree say when it got knocked over?
I'm pine.

What did one snowman say to the other?
Smoking is bad for you.

This intersection has some serious problems. All the signs are there.

Let's talk about the elephant in the room...
Where did he hide the money?
In his trunk

The kid was pretty bland.
I called him matte.

Through a series of lab tests, the jokes just couldn't get a reaction.

I told my kids the Ice Cream Truck only plays music when it's out of ice cream...
Problem solved.

How do you take down a giraffe?
Go for the throat.

Back in my day, Yahoo is the way we used to google something.

Santa and his wife got a divorce; Semicolons are great for separating independent clauses.

Our computer lab is all dark and cramped. It's an Apple lab, so we don't use windows.

The bird flew for hours and days. She sore.

It's easy to see the difference between an outlaw and a child. Outlaws are wanted.

I stole my brother's batteries, but they didn't work. They were free of charge.

You look like a beaver, 'cuz damn.

What do you call a cow after it's been tipped over?
Ground Beef

Do you know what invention broke the most ground in the last 100 years?
A shovel

What does the dog want
for breakfast?
Woofles

I hope you have a Gouda day!
Was that too cheesy?

At the science fair, I used a lime
to power a lightbulb.
Then I basked in the limelight.

Do you know why I like video game jokes? They work on so many levels.

I have a fear of steep hills, and I'll never get over it.

If you want to have a happy life, it's important to start each day with cheerio's.

Why was the gangster's gun leaking?
It's a little uzi.

I know I say I love you most, but really I have no favorites between you kids. I didn't like any of you very much.

Little known fact? A golf course has 18 holes because you'll lose your mind if you only put your balls into 1 hole for the rest of your life.

No honey, I can't hear you when I'm ignoring you.

Your the best thing that ever happened to me. You're all that really matters. You and "Bell's" seasonal IPA.

I refuse to swim in trunks! Cars aren't made for that kind of thing.

All I need to have a good time is a solid fishing rod, a fresh case of Budweiser, and a cabin where I can leave my wife.

All the best things come from long lines. I met your mother in line at the store. I had to wait in line to get my degree, and this one time, I even got a free burrito.

I found an animal covered in cheese, deep under a pile of tortillas.
I called it a quesadilla.

The dog was a nymphomaniac.
He had to go to the pound.

If an unstoppable force meets an immovable object, God must have hit your mother.

What would you call a building designed to make satellites?
Satisfactory

"Just do it" was taken by Nike from the last words of an executed prisoner. He was electrocuted.
All he needed was a rubber soul.

Though I drive through the valley of the shadow of death, I fear no evil, for your mother's not driving.

I'm a tough act to follow,
like Pepe le Pew.

I believe in you, and I'm sure you'll be a great garbage man someday!

If you have 12 pizza rolls thawed on a plate which take 5 minutes to make, and 6 pizza rolls on another plate that are frozen and take 9 minutes to make, can you figure out how long you'll be doing dishes?

We had television remotes in the 50's; We just yelled: "Honey change the channel!"

Why can't Ford beat Dodge?
They can't hit 'em.

You're like a 12 gauge, bangin'.

I'm exhausted!
Are you tired or did you fart?

I may be short, but I'm on the rise!

I don't cry. As a man, they remove our tear ducts at birth.

I took my meds this morning. Three doses!

I don't want to change the world. I just want it to change for the better regardless of my actions.

Get back in line; you're not perpendicular.

If a penguin gets a cold, you might say it flu.

Call me McDonald's because I'm loving it.

Call me BK, because we're doing it my way.

I know my windows better than Microsoft.

What does a pissed off bird say? What the fawks?

Never trust science... It makes up everything.

"I'll call you tonight." That's not my name.

Against criticism that it should be stopped, they released the Mario beer anyway with the statement "It's a can!"

Cars can only drive so far before they tire.

Your dog could get really hurt defending you, but luckily it can heel.

What do you call a perplexed insect?
Beemused

Alexander Hamilton lost every debate to Aaron Burr. Take gun control for instance.

The square says to the circle "You're pointless."

The circle says to the square "Lets roll!"

I told them a story of a UFO, but it went over their head.

The Burgler got caught when he got tangled up in old 50's movies reels. He got caught on tape.

I need some ice water because I'm super-hot.

The satellite was way too late for the wedding, but he made the reception.

HAPPY FATHER'S DAY!

Made in the USA
Middletown, DE
05 June 2018